After Jesus had been crucified, Joseph and Nicodemus, two of his friends, wrapped up his body and buried it in a garden cave. They rolled a great stone across the opening. Soldiers stood guard in case of trouble.

The disciples, and some of the others who had loved Jesus, went back to the room where they had had the special supper. They felt scared and very sad.

But very early on Sunday morning some of the women took oils and spices to put on the body of Jesus. They went out into the dark, silent streets. They knew that Jesus' body had been put into a cave. But there had not been time to do things properly.

4

The women went quietly into the garden.

They wondered how they would get into the cave. But as they came near, they gasped with surprise. The enormous stone had been rolled away from the opening and the guards had gone.

The women ran and peered into the
cave. It was empty! Whatever had
happened? They began to feel worried.

At that moment they saw two men, in
bright, shining clothes, standing beside
the cave. The women could hardly
believe their eyes.

'Why are you looking for Jesus here?' the angels asked. 'He is alive! Don't you remember how he told you that he would be killed but would come back to life again? Run and tell the disciples.'

The women ran back through the city streets, as fast as they could go.

'Jesus is alive — the angels of God have spoken to us,' they gasped to each other as they ran.

When the women arrived at the room
where the others were, they banged on
the door as hard as they could.

'Open the door,' they called to the
disciples. 'We have the best news you've
ever heard. Jesus is alive!'

That same day, two of Jesus' friends were walking home to Emmaus. They did not know that Jesus was alive.

'There's no reason to stay in Jerusalem now that Jesus is dead,' they said. 'We're going home.'

As they walked down the road, another man caught up with them. He did not seem to know what had been happening, so they told him about Jesus' death.

To their surprise, the man began to explain to them why Jesus had to die.

'Come in and have some supper,' they said to him, when they reached home.

At the supper table the visitor took the bread, thanked God for it and began to share it around. Then, at last, they knew who he was. It had been Jesus all the time!

But as soon as they recognized him, he disappeared.

'We must go back to Jerusalem at once and tell the others,' they said.

Although it was night-time they hurried back to Jerusalem.

13

When the two friends arrived, they heard what had happened when the women went to the cave.

'We didn't believe them,' said Simon Peter and John, 'but when we went to the garden we found that it was true. Jesus really is alive.'

14

While the disciples were talking together, Jesus himself came into the room. They all gasped and backed away.

'It's all right,' Jesus said. 'I'm not a ghost, and I would like something to eat.'

The disciples watched him eat some supper. It was wonderful to see Jesus again.

But one disciple was missing. Thomas had not been there to see Jesus.

When they all told him that Jesus was alive, Thomas said, 'I will not believe it until I see him with my own eyes and touch the place where the nails went.'

The very next Sunday, they were all together and Thomas was with them. Jesus came again.

'Here I am, Thomas,' he said quietly. 'Reach out and touch me. Now will you believe that I really am alive?'

'I do believe,' said Thomas. 'You are my Lord and my God.'

After this, Jesus' friends went home to
Lake Galilee. One morning they were out
fishing in their boat. They had fished all
night, but still the nets were empty.

Suddenly a man called out from the
beach, 'Let down the nets on the other
side of the boat.'

'Does he think we don't know how to
fish?' they said. But they did as they
were told. Soon the nets were bulging
with enormous fish.

'It's Jesus!' they all shouted.

That morning, as they had breakfast
together, Jesus had a quiet word with
Peter. He was forgiven for that dreadful
morning when he had said he did not
know Jesus. And he was told he had
special work to do.

Six weeks went by, and Jesus took his disciples for a walk up the hill outside Jerusalem.

'You have seen how God gave me power to heal sick people and give life to those who were dead,' Jesus said. 'You have heard all about God's kingdom.'

'Now it's time for me to go back to my
Father. I want you to tell everyone about
me.

'Go to Jerusalem and wait there. For
God will give you the same power that
he gave me.'

Then the clouds came down, and
when they cleared, Jesus had gone.

The disciples went back to Jerusalem, and waited.

They prayed to God, as Jesus had taught them. They talked of all the wonderful things they had seen and heard while they had been with Jesus.

They did not know it, but an exciting new life was about to begin.

23

The Lion Story Bible is made up of 52 individual stories for young readers, building up an understanding of the Bible as one story — God's story — a story for all time and all people.

The New Testament section (numbers 31–52) covers the life and teaching of God's Son, Jesus. The stories are about the people he met, what he did and what he said. Almost all we know about the life of Jesus is recorded in the four Gospels — Matthew, Mark, Luke and John. The word gospel means 'good news'.
    The last four stories in this section are about the first Christians, who started to tell others the 'good news', as Jesus had commanded them — a story which continues today all over the world.

The story of *The first Easter* is told in all four New Testament Gospels: Matthew, chapter 28; Mark, chapter 16; Luke, chapter 24; John, chapter 20. The ascension is in Acts, chapter 1.
    To the disciples, Jesus' death seemed like the end of the world. They had been looking forward to the coming of God's kingdom — but the King was dead. Nothing made sense. One of them had betrayed Jesus; and Peter had denied he knew him.
    Then, on the Sunday morning, the women found the stone rolled back from the grave and the body gone. By the end of that day they all knew that Jesus was alive again. They had all seen him. Everything he had told them, all he had promised, was true. He had conquered death. He had paid the penalty for sin — for everyone. Now there was good news — the offer of a new life, a fresh start — to share with the whole world.
    The next book in the series, number 49: *Good news for everyone*, tells how that sharing began.